The Story of a Special Day
Volume 72

March 12

71st day of the year
(72nd in leap years)
294 days remaining
until the end of the year.

by Michael Dobson

Timespinner
Press

For more information about the series, about me, or about your special day, please email us at editor@timespinnerpress.com.

Look for other volumes in *The Story of a Special Day,* coming often.

Table of Contents

March 12 Quotations 2

Event of the Day.. 3

March 12 Holidays and Celebrations.............. 6

What Happened on March 12?........................ 9

Who Was Born on March 12? 18

Who Died on March 12? 42

March: The Third Month 57

March Symbols 58

March Events 60

March Zodiac Signs 63

What Day of the Week is March 12? 66

Copyright, Credit, and Contact 68

Cover: Bess Truman, First Lady, receives an award from a delegation of Girl Scouts for serving as the organization's honorary president, in honor of the founding of the first U.S. Girl Scout troop, March 12, 1912.

Back Cover: The month of March, from the French Gothic illuminated manuscript *Les Très Riches Heures du duc de Berry.*

March 12 Quotations

"I believe in an America where millions of Americans believe in an America that's the America millions of Americans believe in. That's the America I love."

— Mitt Romney, born March 12, 1947

"Good writers define reality; bad ones merely restate it."

— Edward Albee, born March 12, 1928

"All of life is a foreign country."

— Jack Kerouac, born March 12, 1922

"Music is your own experience, your own thoughts, your wisdom. If you don't live it, it won't come out of your horn."

— Charlie Parker, died March 12, 1955

Girl Scouts of the USA Founded

In 1899, British General Robert Baden-Powell, surrounded by a Boer army during the Siege of Mafeking, was reportedly impressed with the Mafeking Cadet Corps, a group of boys below fighting age. Mafeking Cadets stood guard, served as messengers and hospital orderlies, and did whatever else they could to allow the adult men to fight. The siege lasted 217 days, and at the end Baden-Powell was a national hero.

In 1907, Baden-Powell organized the first Scouting encampment and established many of the customs and procedures still used by Scouts today. In 1908, Baden-Powell wrote *Scouting for Boys,* using the Mafeking story as an example in the very first chapter. It became the fourth-bestselling book of all time, and the Boy Scout movement spread throughout the British empire. By 1910, many countries, including the United States, had Boy Scouts.

Girls were equally interested in scouting from the very beginning. Baden-Powell and his sister Agnes started the Girl Guides in 1910, and within a year, American Juliette Gordon Low, then living in Scotland, became active in the Girl Guides, forming a Scottish chapter in 1911.

On March 12, 1912, Low founded the first American chapter of the Girl Guides in Savannah, Georgia. The name changed to Girl Scouts of the USA in 1915, and by 1916, there were over 7,000 members.

Low died in 1923, but the movement she began continued to grow. Today, that single chapter of Girl Guides has grown into a national organization with well over 2 million members.

Girl Scouts empowers girls and teaches values including honesty, fairness, courage, compassion, character, sisterhood, confidence, and citizenship. Girl Scouts participate in camping, community service, and other activities. Today, Girl Scouts of the USA is ranked as the 8th most popular charity and nonprofit in America.

Girl Scouts have been leaders in inclusion, admitting girls with disabilities early in its history when they were denied inclusion in most other activities. While Girl Scout troops were originally segregated by race, by the 1950s, the organization changed so successfully that Dr. Martin Luther King, Jr., described the organization as a "force for desegregation."

Girl Scouts of the USA founder Juliette Gordon Low with Scouts

March 12 Holidays and Celebrations

Girl Scout Birthday (United States)

Girl Scout Birthday, held annually on March 12, celebrates the establishment of the first Girl Guide troop in the United States in 1912. (Also see Girl Scout Week in March multi-day events.)

World Day Against Cyber Censorship (Worldwide)

On March 12, 2008, the organizations Reporters Without Borders and Amnesty International declared World Day Against Cyber Censorship. Each March 12, the Netizen Prize is awarded.

Arbor Day (植树节, 植樹節) (China and Taiwan)

The tree-planting holiday known as Arbor Day was first established in the United States in 1872 and is now celebrated in many countries. The Republic of China (Taiwan) established Arbor Day on March 12 in 1927 in honor of Sun Yat-sen. In 1981, the People's Republic of China also established an Arbor Day equivalent on the same date, with legal penalties for those who fail to plant their quota of trees.

National Day (Mauritius)

Mauritius, an island nation in the Indian Ocean, celebrates its independence from Britain (March 12, 1968) and its establishment as a republic (March 12, 1992) on March 12.

Youth Day (Zambia)

On March 12, the southern African country of Zambia celebrates Youth Day.

Christian Feast Days

Saints commemorated on March 12 include Fina, Maximilian the Martyr, Pope Gregory I, and Theophanes the Confessor.

Graekarismessa (Faroe Islands)

The Faroe Islands, an island group roughly halfway between Norway and Iceland, is a self-governing country under the nominal jurisdiction of Denmark. On March 12, they celebrate *Graekarismessa*, the Mass of St. Gregory, which is also the traditional day that the oystercatcher *(tjaldur)*, the Faroes' national bird, returns to the islands.

A Eurasian Oystercatcher *(haematopus ostralegus)* flying in the
Faroe Islands

What Happened on March 12?

538 CE - End of the Siege of Rome

On March 12, 538, Vitiges, king of the Ostrogoths, ended his year-long siege of Rome and retreated to Ravenna, giving the victory to the famous Byzantine general Belisarius in a key moment of the Gothic War of 535 to 554 CE.

1550 CE - Battle of Penco

On March 12, 1550, a force of 200 Spaniards and 300 Mapochoe Indians under Pedro de Validivia defeated 60,000 Mapuche (modern historians think 6,000 is a more accurate number) in what is now modern Chile.

1689 CE - Williamite War in Ireland

Mostly Catholic forces in Ireland fought for Catholic monarch James II ("Jacobites") against Protestant king William of Orange ("Williamites") over who would be King of England, Scotland, and Ireland. William and Mary won the war and the throne; a side effect was that English domination over Ireland was entrenched for a century or more.

Pedro de Valdivia, painted by Federico de Madrazo

1868 CE - Attempted Assassination of Prince Alfred

On March 12, 1868, Henry O'Farrell became the first Australian to attempt a political assassination when he shot Prince Alfred, son of Queen Victoria. Alfred recovered and returned to England; O'Farrell was hanged.

1894 CE - Coca-Cola® In Bottles

Local soda fountain operator Joseph Biedenharn of Vicksburg, Mississippi, was the first person to bottle and sell Coca-Cola®, on March 12, 1894.

1913 CE - Canberra Day

Lady Denman, wife of the Governor-General of Australia, gave the new Australian capital its official name, Canberra, in a ceremony held on March 12, 1913. Canberra Day is celebrated on the second Monday of March each year.

1918 CE - Moscow Becomes Capital of Russia

On March 12, 1918, Moscow once again became the official capital of Russia, ending a period of 215 years in which St. Petersburg held the honor.

1928 CE - St. Francis Dam Disaster

The St. Francis Dam, located about 40 miles northwest of Los Angeles, California, collapsed just before midnight on March 12, 1928, releasing over 12 billion gallons of water in a flood wave over 130 feet high, killing more than 600 people in one of the worst civil engineering failures of the 20th cetury, and the second-greatest loss of life in California history after the 1906 San Francisco Earthquake.

1930 CE - The Salt March Begins

On March 12, 1930, Mahatma Gandhi challenged the British salt monopoly in colonial India by leading a 24-day, 240-mile long march to the sea, where he and his followers made salt without paying the necessary tax. Gandhi himself was arrested, along with over 80,000 other Indians, but the long-range effect of the Salt March was to legitimize Gandhi's movement in world opinion, with lasting effects on the Indian independence movement.

Gandhi (center) during the Salt March, 1930

1933 CE - **First "Fireside Chat"**

Newly-elected President Franklin Roosevelt took office on March 4, 1933, and made his first radio address to the public on Sunday, March 12, 1933, on the subject of the bank crisis. This would be the first of thirty radio programs by the President, which collectively became known as the "fireside chats."

FDR giving a fireside chat

1938 CE - Anschluß Österreichs

The "Anschluss," the occupation and annexation of Austria into Nazi Germany, took place on March 12, 1938.

1940 CE - End of the Winter War

On March 12, 1940, Finland and the Soviet Union signed the Moscow Peace Treaty, ending the Winter War between the two countries. Although the treaty ceded parts of Finland to the Soviet Union, it preserved Finland's independence.

1947 CE - Cold War Begins

President Harry Truman established the Truman Doctrine in a speech on March 12, 1947. It established "the policy of the United States to support free people who are resisting attempted subjugation by armed minorities or by outside presssures," primarily referring to Soviet expansion. It is therefore known as the start of the Cold War, which lasted until the collapse of the Soviet Union in 1991.

1971 CE - Coup d'État in Turkey

Unlike the traditional military coup d'état, involving the movement of tanks and troops, the 1971 Turkish coup was accomplished by sending the "March 12 Memorandum" to the prime minister, laying out an ultimatum.

1993 CE - Bombay Bombings

On Friday, March 12, 1993, 13 bomb explosions took place in Bombay (Mumbai), India, killing 250 and injuring 700. It was carried out by an organized crime syndicate known as "D-Company," evidently in response to the destruction of the Babri Mosque by Hindu extremists the previous December.

1994 CE - Bernie Madoff Pleads Guilty

On March 12, 2009, disgraced financier and Ponzi schemer Bernard Madoff pled guilty to 11 felony counts related to his $65 billion scam, the largest financial fraud in U.S. history. He was sentenced to 150 years in prison and given a $17 billion fine.

2011 CE - Fukushima Reactor Explosion

The massive earthquake and tsunami that hit Japan on March 11, 2011, did major damage to the Fukushima Daiichi Nuclear Power Plant (福島第一原子力発電所) by destroying the emergency generators designed to cool the reactors. The following day, the core of Fukushima Power Plant I melted down, resulting in a explosion that collapsed the concrete building surrounding the reactor vessel and released some radioactive steam into the atmosphere.

Fukushima Reactor I showing leaking steam

Who Was Born on March 12?

The abbreviation "O.S." on some dates refers to the fact that the Russian Empire did not switch from the Julian to the Gregorian calendar at the same time as the rest of Europe, and therefore some figures have two dates for their birth or death.

People whose original names are not in the Western alphabet have their native names in the appropriate script shown in parenthesis.

Acting and Modeling

Tyler Patrick Jones (March 12, 1994 —)

Tyler Patrick Jones appeared as Ned Banks on the CBS series *Ghost Whisperer* for the first two seasons.

Jaimie Alexander (March 12, 1984 —)

Jaimie Alexander appeared in the television series *KyleXY* and the superhero film *Thor.*

Samm Levine (March 12, 1982 —)

Samm Levine appeared in the TV series *Freaks and Geeks* and the film *Inglorious Basterds*.

John-Paul Lavosier (March 12, 1980 —)

Lavosier played Rex Balsom on the ABC soap opera *One Life to Live*.

Rhys Coiro (March 12, 1979 —)

Corio is best known for his role as Billy Marsh on the HBO series *Entourage*.

Masuimi Max (March 12, 1978 —)

Masuimi Max is a fire performer, burlesque dancer, fetish and pinup model, and reality show contestant.

Aaron Eckhart (March 12, 1969 —)

Aaron Eckhart won a Golden Globe nomination for Best Actor for his role in *Thank You for Smoking*, and appeared as Two-Face in *The Dark Knight*.

Julia Campbell (March 12, 1962 —)

Julia Campbell played the "mean girl" role in *Romy and Michele's High School Reunion*.

Titus Welliver (March 12, 1961 —)

Actor Titus Welliver has had featured roles in *Deadwood, Lost, Suns of Anarchy, The Good Wife*, and numerous films.

Courtney B. Vance (March 12, 1960 —)

Vance was a regular on *Law & Order: Criminal Intent* as Assistant DA Ron Carver.

Ron Jeremy (March 12, 1953 —)

Ron Jeremy is famous for his roles in over 2,000 adult films, and has also appeared in the television series *The Surreal Life*.

Jon Provost (March 12, 1950 —)

As a child actor, Jon Provost played Timmy in the CBS television series *Lassie*.

Joe Unger (March 12, 1949 —)

Joe Unger appeared in the horror films *A Nightmare on Elm Street* and *Leatherface: The Texas Chainsaw Massacre II*, among other films.

Frank Welker (March 12, 1946 —)

Frank Welker is the voice of Fred Jones and the eponymous dog in *Scooby-Doo, Where Are You!*

Liza Minnelli (March 12, 1946 —)

Actress, singer, and dancer Liza Minnelli starred in *Cabaret, Arthur*, and many other movies, and is one of the few entertainers to have won an Oscar, an Emmy, a Grammy, and a Tony. She is the daughter of Judy Garland.

Barbara Feldon (March 12, 1933 —)

Barbara Feldon is best known as Agent 99 in the sitcom *Get Smart* (below, with Don Adams)

Billie "Buckwheat" Thomas (March 12, 1931 — October 10, 1980)

As a child actor, Billie Thomas played Buckwheat in the long-running *Our Gang/Little Rascals* series of short films.

Gordon MacRae (March 12, 1921 — January 24, 1986)

Gordon MacRae appeared in 1955's *Oklahoma* and 1956's *Carousel*, along with many other musicals.

Googie Withers (March 12, 1917 — July 15, 2011)

English actress Googie Withers's memorable roles include supporting roles in Hitchcock's *The Lady Vanishes*, the 1942 film *One of Our Aircraft is Missing*, and the 1950 film *Night and the City*.

Business

Herb Kelleher (March 12, 1931 —)

Herb Kelleher co-founded and served as chairman and CEO of Southwest Airlines.

Gianni Agnelli (March 12, 1921 — January 24, 2003)

Gianni Agnelli was the head of Fiat from 1966 to 1996.

George W. Mason (March 12, 1891 — October 9, 1954)

Mason was chairman and CEO of the Nash-Kelvinator Corporation and CEO of American Motors from 1928 to his death in 1954.

Lane Kirkland (March 12, 1922 — August 14, 1999)

Labor leader Lane Kirkland was president of the AFL-CIO for over 16 years.

Clement Studebaker (March 12, 1831 — November 27, 1901)

Clement Studebaker began making Conestoga wagons, and after his death, his company moved into automobiles, making Studebaker the only manufacturer of horse-drawn vehicles to make the switch to cars successfully.

Crime

Benjamin Arellano Félix (March 12, 1952 —)

A drug trafficker and former leader of the Tijuana Cartel, Félix was extradited to the U.S., convicted of racketeering and conspiracy, and sentenced to 25 years.

Sammy "The Bull" Gravano (March 12, 1945 —)

Underboss of the Gambino crime family, Gravano became an FBI witness and helped bring down the family's boss, John Gotti

Ratko Mladić (Ратко Младић) (March 12, 1942 —)

Bosnian Serb military leader Ratko Mladić was charged with crimes against humanity and genocide before the International Criminal Tribunal at The Hague for his role in the Yugoslav Wars.

Music and Dance

Christina Grimmie (March 12, 1994 —)

Singer/songwriter Christina Grimmie (zeldaxlove64) got her start on YouTube, gaining over 289 million views and 1.5 million subscribers, before being signed to a contract.

Holly Williams (March 12, 1981 —)

Country singer Holly Williams is the granddaughter of Hank Williams, the daughter of Hank Williams Jr., and the half-sister of Hank Williams III.

Marlon Jackson (March 12, 1957 —)

Marlon Jackson was a member of the Jackson 5.

Steve Harris (March 12, 1956 —)

Steve Harris founded the British heavy metal band Iron Maiden.

Randy Stonehill (March 12, 1952 —)

Randy Stonehill is known as one of the pioneers of contemporary Christian music.

Bill Payne (March 12, 1949 —)

Bill Payne co-founded the rock band Little Feat.

Al Jarreau (March 12, 1940 —)

Jazz and pop singer Al Jarreau won seven Grammys in his distinguished career.

Lew DeWitt (March 12, 1938 —)

Country music tenor Lew DeWitt sang with the Statler Brothers and wrote such hits as "Flowers on the Wall."

James Taylor (March 12, 1948 —)

James Taylor (above) is a five-time Grammy winner and a member of the Rock & Roll Hall of Fame. His hits include "Fire and Rain," "You've Got a Friend," "Handy Man," and "Don't Let Me Be Lonely Tonight."

Georges Delerue (March 12, 1925 — March 20, 1992)

French composer George Delerue scored over 350 movies and television shows. He won an Academy Award for *A Little Romance*, and was nominated an additional four times.

Agathe von Trapp (March 12, 1913 — December 28, 2010)

A member of the Trapp Family Singers, Agathe was the model for the character Liesl in the film *The Sound of Music*.

Vaslav Nijinsky (Ва́цлав Нижи́нский) (March 12, 1889 — April 8, 1950)

Legendary ballet dancer Nijinsky began with the Ballets Russe and went on his own after his marriage. He became mentally unstable in later years, and was unable to dance again in public.

Thomas Arne (March 12, 1710 — March 5, 1778)

British composer Thomas Arne is best known for the patriotic song "Rule, Britannia!," for an early version of "God Save the King," which became Britain's national anthem, and for "A-Hunting We Will Go."

Nijinsky in the ballet "Le Festin," approximately 1910

Politics

Tammy Duckworth (March 12, 1968 —)

Iraq war helicopter pilot Tammy Duckworth lost both her legs in conflict, and was elected to the House of Representatives from Illinois's 8th Congressional District.

David Mellor (March 12, 1949 —)

British politician David Mellor is Secretary of State for National Heritage, and served as Chief Secretary to the Treasury.

Mitt Romney (March 12, 1947 —)

Mitt Romney (left) is a former governor of Massachusetts and was the 2012 Republican nominee for President of the United States.

Andrew Young (March 12, 1932 —)

Civil rights activist and former pastor Andrew Young was U.S. Ambassador to the United Nations, mayor of Atlanta, Georgia, and a member of the House of Representatives.

Win Tin (ဝင်းတင်) (March 12, 1929 —)

Burmese political prisoner and leader of the National League for Democracy Win Tin was freed after 19 years in prison for his political actions.

Raúl Alfonsín (March 12, 1936 —)

Alfonsín was president of Argentina from 1983 to 1989.

William Dudley Pelley (March 12, 1890 — June 30, 1965)

Extremist and spiritualist William Pelley founded the pro-fascist Silver Legion in 1933 and ran for President in 1936 on the Christian Party ticket. He was charged with high treason and sedition for his activities during World War II and sentenced to 15 years.

Charles Boycott (March 12, 1832 — June 19, 1897)

When the Irish Land League called for the isolation of British land agent Charles Boycott from the community around him, the resultant press coverage led to the widespread adoption of the word "boycott."

Jane Pierce (March 12, 1806 — December 2, 1863)

Jane Pierce was First Lady of the United States from 1853 to 1857 as the wife of President Franklin Pierce.

Science and Space

Leo Esaki (江崎 玲於奈)(March 12, 1925 —)

Japanese physicist Leo Esaki shared the 1973 Nobel Prize for his discovery of electron tunneling. He invented the Esaki diode.

Wally Schirra (March 12, 1923 — May 3, 2007)

Astronaut Wally Schirra (right) is the only person to have flown in all three of America's space programs Mercury, Gemini, and Apollo, logging nearly 300 hours in space.

Simon Newcomb (March 12, 1835 — July 11, 1909)

Astronomer and mathematician Simon Newcomb's work at the U.S. Naval Observatory in measuring the position of the planets led to his appointment as director of the Nautical Almanac Office. He was buried with military honors at Arlington National Cemetery.

Gustav Kirchoff (March 12, 1824 — October 17, 1887)

German physicist Gustav Kirchoff coined the term "black body radition" and developed "Kirchoff's laws" in circuit theory, thermal emission, and thermochemistry.

Sports

Tyler Clary (March 12, 1989 —)

Clary won the gold medal in the 200-meter backstroke at the 2012 Summer Olympics.

Jessica Hardy (March 12, 1987 —)

Jessica Hardy won a gold in the 4x100-meter relays at the 2012 Summer Olympics, and achieved world records in the 50-meter and 100-meter breaststroke.

Shaun Rogers (March 12, 1979 —)

Defensive tackle Shaun Rogers was a three-time Pro Bowl selection, and played for the Detroit Lions, Cleveland Browns, New Orleans Saints, and New York Giants.

Isaiah Rider (March 12, 1971 —)

Shooting guard Isaiah Rider was NBA Slam-Dunk champion in 1994, Big West Conference Player of the Year in 1993, and played for several NBA teams in an eight year career marred by brushes with the law.

Steve Finley (March 12, 1965 —)

Outfielder Steve Finley won the Gold Glove Award five times in his MLB career.

Grant Long (March 12, 1966 —)

NBA player Grant Long is one of the few players to have played in over 1,000 NBA games.

Darryl Strawberry (March 12, 1962 —)

Outfielder Darryl Strawberry was known for his home runs and for various legal and personal problems off the field.

Matt Millen (March 12, 1958 —)

Former NFL linebacker Matt Millen played on four Super Bowl-winning teams, CEO of the Detroit Lions, and a football commentator for several national television and radio networks.

Dale Murphy (March 12, 1956 —)

MLB outfielder and first baseman Dale Murphy won two consecutive National League MVP Awards, four straight Silver Slugger Awards, and five straight Gold Glove Awards.

Jimmy Wynn (March 12, 1942 —)

Nicknamed "Toy Cannon," Jimmy Wynn played for the Houston Colt .45/Astros, Los Angeles Dodgers, Atlanta Braves, New York Yankees, and the Milwaukee Brewers in his 15 year career.

Johnny Rutherford (March 12, 1938 —)

Automobile racer Johnny Rutherford is one of only nine drivers to win the Indianapolis 500 at least three times. He is a member of the Motorsports Hall of Fame of America, the National Sprint Car Hall of Fame, and the International Motorsports Hall of Fame.

Eddie Sutton (March 12, 1936 —)

In his 36-year Division I basketball coaching career, Eddie Sutton is one of only eight major college men's basketball coaches to have over 800 career wins.

Vernon Law (March 12, 1930 —)

In his 16 season career with the Pittsburgh Pirates, pitcher Vernon Law won the Cy Young Award, the Lou Gehrig Memorial Award, and was 1965's NL Comeback Player of the Year.

Writing and Journalism

David Eggers (March 12, 1970 —)

David Eggers hit the best-seller list with his memoir *A Heartbreaking Work of Staggering Genius*, which won the Pulitzer Prize, and has also won numerous awards for *What is the What: The Autobiography of Valentino Achak Deng*.

Jake Tapper (March 12, 1969 —)

ABC and CNN journalist Jake Tapper wrote *The Outpost: An Untold Story of American Valor*, which became a New York *Times* bestseller.

Steve Levy (March 12, 1965 —)

ESPN journalist Steve Levy is known as "Mr. Overtime" for calling the three longest televised games in NHL history.

Carl Hiassen (March 12, 1953 —)

Florida novelist Carl Hiassen is best known for his 1993 book *Strip Tease*, which became a movie starring Demi Moore and Burt Reynolds.

Naomi Shihab Nye (نعومي شهاب ناي) (March 12, 1952 —)

Palestinian-American poet and novelist Naomi Shihab Nye won four Pushcart Prizes, the Jane Addams Children's Book Award, and the 2013 NSK Neustadt Prize for Children's Literature.

Lloyd Dobyns (March 12, 1936 —)

NBC news correspondent Lloyd Dobyns won 28 national awards including a George Foster Peabody Medal for his work as a television journalist, host, and reporter.

Edward Albee (March 12, 1928 —)

Playwright Edward Albee is best known as the author of *Who's Afraid of Virginia Woolf?*

Harry Harrison (March 12, 1925 — August 15, 2012)

Science fiction writer Harry Harrison is best known for his long-running character the Stainless Steel Rat and for his 1966 novel *Make Room! Make Room!*, which formed the rough basis for the 1973 motion picture *Soylent Green*.

Jack Kerouac (March 12, 1922 — October 21, 1969)

Beat Generation legend Jack Kerouac is best known for his 1957 book *On the Road*.

Jack Kerouac

Millard Kaufman (March 12, 1917 — March 4, 2009)

Screenwriter and novelist Millard Kaufman is known for writing the Academy-nominated *Bad Day at Black Rock*, and as one of the creators of the nearsighted cartoon character Mr. Magoo.

Adolph Ochs (March 12, 1858 — April 8, 1935)

Adolph Ochs was owner and publisher of the New York *Times* from 1896 until his death.

Bishop Berkeley (March 12, 1685 — January 14, 1753)

George Berkeley, Bishop of Cloyne, was an Anglo-Irish philosopher who developed the idea of "immaterialism." He coined the famous phrase *esse est percipi* ("to be is to be perceived").

John Aubrey (March 12, 1626 — June 7, 1697)

Natural philosopher and writer John Aubrey is best known as the author of a collection of short biographical pieces known as *Brief Lives*. As an archeologist, he discovered the Avebury henge monument.

Geo. Berkeley S.T.P.
Dec. Deronfis.

Bishop Berkeley by John Smybert

Who Died on March 12?

Acting and Television

Lynne Thigpen (December 22, 1948 — March 12, 2003)

Lynn Thigpen was best known as "The Chief" in the television shows based on *Where in the World is Carmen Santiago?*

Morton Downey, Jr. (December 9, 1932 — March 12, 2001)

Talk show host Morton Downey, Jr., pioneered the "trash TV" format on the eponymous *The Morton Downey Jr. Show.*

Maurice Evans (June 3, 1901 — March 12, 1989)

Shakespearean actor Maurice Evans is perhaps best known as Dr. Zaius in *Planet of the Apes* and as the father of Samantha in the TV series *Bewitched.*

Maurice Evans

John Cazale (August 12, 1935 — March 12, 1978)

John Cazale is best known for his role as Fredo in the first two *Godfather* films.

Art

Beatrice Wood (March 3, 1893 — March 12, 1998)

Artist and potter Beatrice Wood was known as the "Mama of Dada" and was a partial inspiration for the character of "Rose" in the 1997 film *Titanic*.

Illarion Pryanishnikov (Илларио́н Пря́нишников) (March 20 [O.S. April 1], 1940 — March 12 [O.S. March 24], 1894)

Russian painter Illarion Pryanishnikov was one of the founders of the Peredvizhniki artistic cooperative in Russia.

William James Blacklock (March 3, 1816 — March 12, 1858)

English landscape painter William James Blacklock was an important transition figure between 19th century Romanticism and the Pre-Raphaelite School.

Portrait of Illarion Pryanishnikov by Vasily Perov

Business

Robert Bosch (September 23, 1861 — March 12, 1942)

German engineer and businessman Robert Bosch founded the company named for him. Bosch is the world's largest supplier of automotive components, employing over 300,000 people.

Asa Griggs Candler (December 30, 1851 — March 12, 1929)

Tycoon Asa Griggs Candler made his fortune as the co-founder of Coca-Cola, and also served as mayor of Atlanta from 1916 to 1919.

George Westinghouse (October 6, 1846 — March 12, 1914)

George Westinghouse, founder of the company that bears his name, invented the railway air brake and was one of Thomas Edison's rivals in developing the electricity system in the United States. His alternating current approach won out over Edison's direct current.

George Westinghouse

Crime

Joe Petrosino (August 30, 1860 — March 12, 1909)

New York City police lieutenant Joe Petrosino was an early leader in the fight against organized crime. He helped Enrico Caruso against the Black Hand, uncovered evidence of the plot to assassinate President William McKinley (but the Secret Service ignored him, and the President was assassinated), and arrested Don Vito Cascioferro. Petrosino was killed by Mafia assassins in Palermo, Italy.

Exploration

Alexander Mackenzie (1764 — March 12, 1820)

Sir Alexander Mackenzie made the first overland east-to-west crossing of North America to reach the Pacific Ocean in 1793, predating the Lewis and Clark expedition by ten years.

Music

Michael Hossack (October 17, 1946 — March 12, 2012)

Michael Hossack was the drummer for the Doobie Brothers.

Joe Morello (July 17, 1928 — March 12, 2011)

Jazz drummer Joe Morello is best known for his work with The Dave Brubeck Quartet on classic pieces including "Take Five" and "Blue Rondo à la Turk."

Yehudi Menuhin (April 22, 1916 — March 12, 1999)

Yehudi Menuhin is often listed as one of the greatest violinists of the 20th century.

Eugene Ormandy (November 18, 1899 — March 12, 1985)

Conductor Eugene Ormandy led the Philadelphia Orchestra for 44 years. He received the Presidential Medal of Freedom in 1970.

Charlie Parker (August 29, 1920 — March 12, 1955)

Known as "Yardbird" or "Bird," jazz saxophonist Charlie Parker was a leading figure in the development of bepop and an icon of the Beat Generation.

Charlie Parker (in foreground) with Miles Davis (right). Dizzy Gillespie (with glasses) is visible in the background.

Politics and Military

Victor Sokolov (Виктор Соколов) (February 21, 1947 — March 12, 2006)

Soviet dissident Victor Sokolov was stripped of his Soviet citizenship after moving to the UNited States in 1975.

William George Barker (November 3, 1894 — March 12, 1930)

Canadian World War I fighter ace William George Barker is the most decorated serviceman in the history of the British Empire and Commonwealth of Nations.

Sun Yat-sen (孫文 / 孫逸仙) (February 21, 1947 — March 12, 2006)

Chinese revolutionary Sun Yat-sen was the founder and first president of the Republic of China, overthrowing the Qing dynasty and co founding the Kuomintang.

Cesare Borgia (1475? — March 12, 1507)

Illegitimate son of Pope Alexander VI, brother of Lucrezia Borgia, and member of the powerful Borgia clan, Cesare Borgia was the first person to resign as a cardinal of the Catholic Church. Commanding the papal armies, Borgia took over a large part of Italy, but was unable to retain his position following the death of his father the Pope. He was known as an early patron of Leonardo da Vinci. (Portrait of Cesare Borgia, above, by Altobello Melone.)

Religion

Pope Gregory I (c. 540 — March 12, 604)

Known as Gregory the Great, Pope Gregory I is known for his writings, more prolific than any of his predecessors in office. He was known as the "father of Christian worship" and is considered a saint not only by Catholics by also by Orthodox, Anglican, and some Lutheran denominations. He is also credited with the development of the "Gregorian chant."

Sports

Woody Hayes (February 14, 1913 — March 12, 1987)

College Football Hall of Fame Coach Woody Hayes led the Ohio State Buckeyes for 28 seasons, winning five national championships. He was fired after striking an opposing player during the 1978 Gator Bowl.

Frankie Frisch (September 9, 1898 — March 12, 1973)

Nicknamed the "Fordham Flash," Frankie Frisch played for the New York Giants and St. Louis Cardinals, and later managed the Cardinals, the Pittsburgh Pirates, and the Chicago Cubs. He was inducted into the Baseball Hall of Fame in 1947.

Frank Frisch baseball card

Writing

Howard Fast (November 11, 1914 — March 12, 2003)

Screenwriter and novelist Howard Fast was imprisoned and blacklisted by the House Committee on Un-American Activities during the "Red Scare" of the 1950s. He wrote the screenplay to the movie *Spartacus*, the novels *Citizen Tom Paine* and *Freedom Road*. A long-standing member of the Communist Party, he won the Stalin Peace Prize in 1953.

Robert Ludlum (May 25, 1927 — March 12, 2001)

Best-selling thriller writer Robert Ludlum is best known for *The Bourne Identity* and its sequels.

Winston Churchill (November 10, 1871 — March 12, 1947)

American author Winston Churchill, no relation to the British prime minister, had a successful career as a writer beginning with the 1898 novel *The Celebrity*.

The month of March, from the illuminated manuscript *Les Très Riches Heures du duc de Berry*

March: The Third Month

In ancient Rome, March was the first month of the year. As the first month of spring, in the Mediterranean climate it marked the beginning of the military campaign season. That's why March (Martius) is named in honor of Mars, the Roman god of war.

Although the first month of the year was moved back to January sometime during the transition of Rome from a kingdom to a republic (historians differ), March was the first month of the year in Russia until the end of the 15th Century, and is the first month of the year in many other cultures and religions.

In the northern hemisphere, March 1 marks the beginning of meteorological spring. In the southern hemisphere, March is the equivalent of September, making southern hemisphere March the beginning of autumn.

March is one of the seven months that have 31 days in it. March starts on the same day of the week as November every year, and except for leap years starts on the same day as February. March starts on the same day of the week as the previous June except for leap years, and in leap years starts on the same day as the previous September and December.

March in Other Cultures

In Finland, March is called *maaliskuu* (earthy month). In Ukraine, it's *березень* (birch tree). Other names for March include *Lentmona*t (Saxon), *Hyld-monath* (Angles), and *sušec* (Slovene).

March Symbols

Birthstones: Aquamarine and bloodstone, both representing courage.

Aquamarine

Birth Flowers: Daffodils

Daffodils in Bagatelle Park, Paris, France

March Events

Honorary months: Presidents, Congresses, and nations around the world issue proclamations recognizing particular months to honor certain causes. These events generally fall in March. (All US unless otherwise noted.)

- National Nutrition Month

- American Red Cross Month

- Women's History Month (celebrated in Canada during October)

- Irish-American Heritage Month

- Colorectal Cancer Awareness Month

- Fire Prevention Month (The Philippines)

"March Madness": (United States) The NCAA Men's Division I Basketball Championship, popularly known as "March Madness" or the "Big Dance," is a single-elimination tournament to establish the champion college basketball team.

Multi-day events: Some March events span multiple days.

- **Nineteen Day Fast:** (Bahá'í Faith) March 2 through March 20

- **Girl Scout Week:** (U.S.) The week that includes March 12, the date of the founding of the first chapter of the Girl Scouts of the USA in 1912. The earliest Girl Scout Week can start is March 6, and the latest it can end is March 18. The Sunday of Girl Scout Week is celebrated by some churches as Girl Scout Sunday or Girl Scout Sabbath.

Movable events: Some events change dates from year to year.

- **Commonwealth Day:** Commonwealth Day, formerly Empire Day, celebrates the establishment of the Commonwealth of Nations. It is marked by a service in Westminster Abbey and by a speech by England's monarch to the Commonwealht nations around the world. Commonwealth Day is held annually on the second Monday in March, which can fall on any day between March 8 and March 14.

- **Canberra Day:** In the Australian Capital Territory, Canberra Day celebrates the official naming of Australia's capital city. It is also held annually on the second Monday in March, which can fall on any day between March 8 and March 14.

- **Passion Sunday:** The fifth Sunday of the Christian season of Lent is known as Passion Sunday in various Protestant denominations and by some traditionalist Catholics. Sometimes, the sixth Sunday of Lent is also known as Passion Sunday, but it is more commonly known as Palm Sunday. Passion Sunday starts the two week Passiontide, which ends on Holy Saturday, the day before Easter, commemorating the day that Jesus's body was laid in the tomb. The fifth Sunday of Lent can occur as early as March 8, and as late as April 11.

March Zodiac Signs

From the perspective of someone on Earth, the Sun appears to move through the sky throughout the year, along a path astronomers call the ecliptic plane. The ecliptic plane is divided into twelve constellations, known as the zodiac, based on traditionally observed patterns of stars. On your birthday, you can't see your constellation, because it's part of the daytime sky.

The zodiac was first developed by Babylonian astronomers about 2,500 years ago. Because they were unaware that the Earth wobbles like a spinning top (a motion known as *precession*), they didn't make allowance for the fact that the Sun's path through the zodiac changes over time. That means there are now two sets of dates for your birth sign. The *tropical dates* are the original Babylonian dates; the *siderial dates* tell you where the Sun actually appears as it moves along its annual path.

March 12 is in Pisces in tropical dates, and is in Aquarius in siderial.

Aquarius

Tropical January 20 to February 19

Siderial February 12 to March 14

Aquarius is one of the oldest recognized constellations, originally representing the Babylonian god Ea. In Latin, Aquarius means "water-carrier," represented in its symbol. In Greek mythology, Aquarius is sometimes associated with Deucalion, who survived a world-cleansing flood. In Chinese astronomy, it is known as the Black Tortoise of the North (北方玄武, Běi Fāng Xuán Wǔ).

In astrology, Aquarius is considered to be masculine and extroverted, and despite the name is an air sign. Aquarians are supposed to be philanthropical, inventive, and individualistic.

Pisces

Tropical February 20 to March 20

Siderial March 15 to April 14

In the Roman legend of Venus and her son Cupid, they escaped the clutches of Typhon, known as the "father of all monsters," by transforming into fish and tying themselves together with rope. That's why the name Pisces is plural for fish. The constellation appears as a somewhat ragged "V" shape, representing the rope, with the "fish" located at the two rope ends.

In astrology, Pisces is a water sign, compatible with the other water signs Cancer and Scorpio, as well as with the earth signs Taurus, Virgo, and Capricorn. Pisceans are supposed to be imaginative, compassionate, unworldly, secretive, and escapist.

What Day of the Week is March 12?

On what day of the week does March 12 fall?

Surprisingly, this isn't an easy question. Because the calendar year is 365 days long (366 in leap years), it doesn't divide evenly by the seven days of the week.

Also, the Earth goes around the Sun in about 365-1/4 days, so a calendar tends to drift over time. That's why the same date falls on different weekdays in different years.

This is made even more complicated by a change in calendars that took place in 1582. Our modern calendar has its roots in ancient Rome, in a calendar reform conducted by Julius Caesar. Caesar commissioned mathematicians to attack the problem, and came up with the idea of *leap years*, and thus standardized the calendar for centuries to come. This was called the *Julian calendar.*

Over time, however, the small errors in Caesar's calculation compounded. That's why Pope Gregory XIII commissioned the *Gregorian calendar*, used in most of the world today. Some countries converted in 1582, when the calendar was first developed; some converted later; other still haven't changed.

Gregorian and Julian aren't the only types of calendars. The Hebrew year, the Islamic year, and many other calendars are used in different parts of the world and among different people.

You can convert Gregorian dates to other calendars, including the Hebrew calendar, the Islamic calendar, and even the Mayan calendar by visiting the Fourmilab Calendar Converter at http://www.fourmilab.ch/documents/calendar/.

A 50-year brass perpetual calendar.

Copyright, Credit, and Contact

Follow Us

Our blog Dobson's Improbable History features short articles on events and people associated with each day, and updates several times each week. Get the latest on Twitter @SidewiseThinker.

Sources and Art Credits

All art and photographs are either in the public domain or used under a Creative Commons license. Attribution is provided where requested by the copyright owner or when of historical significance, listed below.

- The photograph of Juliette Gordon Low and two Girl Scouts is in the public domain because its copyright has expired.

- The photograph of the Eurasian Oystercatcher *(haematopus ostralegus)* flying in the Faroe Islands was taken by Ulrich Latzenhofer, and is used under the Creative Commons Attribution-Share Alike 2.0 Generic license.

- The painting of Pedro de Valdivia by Federico de Madrazo hangs in the Mayor's Room of the City of Santiago, Chile. It is the public domain because its copyright has expired.

- The photograph of Gandhi on the Salt March is in the public domain because its copyright has expired.

- The photograph of FDR giving a fireside chat is from the collection of the Franklin Delano Roosevelt Presidential Library, National Archives and Records Administration, and is in the public domain as a work of the U.S. federal government.

- The photograph of the Fukushima I nuclear power plant explosion was taken by Digital Globe, and is used under the Creative Commons Attribution-Share Alike 3.0 Unported license.

- The publicity photograph of Liza Minnelli in *Cabaret* is in the public domain because it was published between 1923 and 1977 without a copyright notice.

- The publicity photograph of Barbara Feldon and Don Adams in *Get Smart* is in the public domain because it was published between 1923 and 1977 without a copyright notice.

- The screenshot of Billie "Buckwheat" Thomas from *Our Gang* is in the public domain because it was published between 1923 and 1977 without a copyright notice.

- The publicity photo of James Taylor is in the public domain because it was published between 1923 and 1977 without a copyright notice.

- The photograph of Vaslav Nijinksy is in the public domain because its copyright has expired.

- The 2011 photograph of Mitt Romney is a crop of an image by Gage Skidmore, and is used here under the terms of the Creative Commons Attribution-Share Alike 3.0 Unported license.

- The photograph of Wally Schirra is in the public domain because it is a work of NASA.

- The 1956 photograph of Jack Kerouac is by Tom Palumbo, and is used here under the terms of the Creative Commons Attribution-Share Alike 2.0 Unported license.

- The painting of Bishop George Berkeley by John Smybert is in the public domain because its copyright has expired. The original is in the collection of the National Portrait Gallery in Washington, DC.

- The publicity photo of Maurice Evans is in the public domain because it was published between 1923 and 1977 without a copyright notice.

- The portrait of Illarion Pryanishnikov by Vasily Perov is in the public domain because its copyright has expired.

- The photograph of George Westinghouse was taken by Joseph G. Gessford. It is part of the Library of Congress

Prints and Photographs Division collection, and is in the public domain because its copyright has expired.

- The photograph of Charlie Parker, Tommy Potter, Miles Davis, Dizzy Gillespie, and Max Roach at the Three Deuces in New York was taken by William P. Gottlieb and is from the William P. Gottlieb Collection at the Library of Congress Music Division. It is in the public domain by the wishes of the photographer.

- Portrait of a Gentleman (Cesare Borgia) by Altobello Melone is in the public domain because its copyright has expired. The original can be seen in the Galleria dell'Accademia Carrara in Bergamo, Italy.

- The Big League Chewing Gum baseball card of Frank Frisch is in the public domain because its copyright was not renewed.

- The illustration of the month of March is from the French Gothic illuminated manuscript *Les Très Riches Heures du duc de Berry* by the Limbourg Brothers, Jean Colombe, and an intermediate painter whose name is lost to history.

- The photograph of aquamarine has been released into the public domain.

- The photograph of daffodils is by Myrabella, and is licensed under the Creative Commons Attribution-Share Alike 3.0 Unported license.

- The 1917 Women's Suffrage demonstration comes from the Library of Congress, Prints and Photographs Division, LC-USZ62-31799 DLC

- The 50-year perpetual calendar photograph is in the public domain.